hanna shebar

For the one that feels *like*

home

poems, letters, confessions

ISBN: 978-1-7378977-8-1

This book is for all my loves.

The past.

The present.

The future.

And the almost…

CONTENTS

Little Bell 9

Strawberries and Pink 11

I Love the World 12

We All Want to Belong 13

My Mother's Love 14

Whisper 17

For You, Who I Am Yet to Meet 18

The Dance 20

Six Thousand Miles 21

Fire and Water 23

Loving a Dream 24

Almost 25

I'm a Crier 26

Is Love Real? 28

Confession 29

The Fear 30

Fate 31

Home 33

September 23rd 34

Matches in the Dark 36

Body 37

Exhausted 38

5 a.m. 39

Almost Right 41

Choose Me Wild 42

Christmas 43

Where Does Love Go? 45

Strangers Again 46

Maybe 48

Imperfect Mess 49

Still a Believer 50

The One Who Stays 52

Light in the Dark 53

CONTENTS

Seen in Full 54
I Don't Need You to Survive 55
A Little Softness 56
October 57
In the Next Life 58
Keeper of Your Dreams 59
Getting Lost to Find You 60
November 61
You Don't Have to Be Perfect 62
Travelers 64
Dancing in the Chaos 65
In Another Timeline 66
"I Love You" Is in Many Things 67
This Chapter 68
Silly Girl 69
Proof That Love Exists 70
June, 2025 72
Special to Me 73
Found Me in Your Eyes 74
Temple 76
I Wish I Could Hate You 77
I Am Not Broken 78
When I Arrive 79
You Will Be Loved 80
I Know What I Want 81
I Was Never a Summer Girl 82
Maybe That's the Point 83
My Final Act of Love 84
Spring 85
The Beauty of Being Human 86
May Love Find You Gently 87
Home 89

"Where thou art—that—is Home."

— Emily Dickinson

for the one
that feels like

Home

Little Bell

That's what my grandma used to call me. It was quite befitting for a child with undiagnosed ADHD.

She would say, "The house comes alive the moment Hanna walks through the door."

And it did.

I danced. I sang. I laughed so loud the neighbors knew I was visiting. I would put on a show and live for the applause and cheering. I played with my dolls and left them scattered around the house, knowing I wouldn't get into trouble for not cleaning up after myself. I knew my grandparents would give me anything I asked for.

I was their Little Bell — someone who turned the house upside down but filled it with joy.

I leapt across rooms with an imagination that had no bounds, inventing stories for my dolls and sending them off on grand adventures. Every inch of the house became my stage. Every corner was a new world to explore. I never slowed down. My mind was always racing ahead of me, dreaming up new games, new ideas, new ways to make everyone smile.

And my grandma loved it. Her eyes would light up every time she saw me, as if something magical had just arrived. She never told me to quiet down. Never asked me to sit still. Instead, she would say, "Let the bell ring as long as it wants."

And that's what I did.

I didn't know then that the whirlwind inside me had a name. To me, it was just how life was meant to be lived — full of noise, laughter, and mess. It wasn't until later, when I was older, that the world began asking me to quiet down, to focus, to fit into a mold that felt too tight around my mind.

But in that house, with my grandma, I was free.

In that home, I will forever remain a little bell.

Strawberries and Pink

I like strawberries and the color pink.
I drink peach wine and eat cherry pie.

My screen time is ten hours a day,
and I rewatch the same movies every year.

My favorite book is still the one I loved at thirteen.

I have a playlist for every mood,
but I always return to the same four songs.

I enjoy caramel ice cream,
and I prefer going to the movies alone.

I keep empty journals
because they are too pretty to be spoiled with ink.

I keep the window open when it rains,
and I still wear the same perfume I did at seventeen.

I don't ask for much—
just a little magic in the ordinary,
and maybe someone
who understands the quiet parts of me

I Love the World

I think I just love the world.
I love life.
I love morning walks and the cold weather.
I love sunny days in the park.
I love the taste of warm, fresh bread and butter.
I love the sound of birds singing outside my bedroom
window.

I love the rain, and I love getting into a warm bed at the
end of the day.

I love people, even the ones I don't get along with.
I love the flowers that bloom in unexpected places.
And I love the way music fills a room.

I think I just love the world.

And I love you…

We All Want to Belong

We all secretly want to belong.
To be seen.
To be heard.
To be loved.

We all secretly want to matter.
To make a difference.
To leave a mark.

We all secretly want to be remembered.
Not for what we have, but for who we are.

My Mother's Love

With age, I realized there is no one as loving as my
mother.

Her heart is so big it could fill the whole world
and still have room for more.

She is the one who cries over movies,
over stories and people she has never met.
The one who would pick up an abandoned kitten left on
her porch
and nurse him back to life,
teaching him what love and home mean.

She is the one chasing a lost dog on the freeway
just to make sure he's okay.
The one who will pray for a boy she's never met,
because maybe no one else is praying for him.

She is the one who gives people everything she has
and never asks for anything in return.

With age, I realized
her love is the purest thing I have ever known.
It is patient.
Forgiving.
Endless like an ocean.

With age, I realized
no one will ever love me the way my mother does.

Her love is the kind that makes you want to be better,
to love as deeply and as selflessly as she does.

If I can live even a fraction of my life
the way she lives hers,
I will consider myself lucky.

Whisper

My heart calls out to yours,
Hoping you will hear—
A silent plea in the stillness,
A whisper drawing near.

I send my thoughts like letters,
Carried by the wind,
Waiting for the moment
Your heart will let them in

For You, Who I am yet to Meet

i'm sorry it's taking me so long
to make my way to you.
i'm sorry i got lost so many times
along the way.

i swear i'm coming.
i swear, i'll make it to you when i am meant to.
i'm still learning, and i am still unlearning
all the things i thought i knew.

sometimes, alone at night,
i wonder if you are searching for me too.
i wonder if you've fought your own battles
and carried your own scars.
i wonder if you think of me too,
alone at night.

I hope you can forgive me
for taking so long to find you—
For every wrong turn,
For every time I thought I had found you
in someone else's eyes,
Only to realize it wasn't you.

For now, I'll keep searching,
keep growing, keep believing
That you are out there, doing the same.

And when we meet,
I hope to tell you
how I knew it was always you

The Dance

I dance for the world.

They call me mad,
and I continue my dance,
hoping
someone will join.

Six Thousand Miles

And maybe
my cry echoes in your heart,

six thousand miles away,

as you lay there
awake at night

I'll recognize your face among millions.

I'll know you in the crowd
before we meet.

My soul will always remember yours.

One lifetime
will never be enough
to love you.

Fire and Water

Maybe you can teach me patience.
For you, I would be willing to learn—
God knows I have none.

I have always been a fire:
Quick to spark, quick to burn.
But maybe you are the water
That soothes my restless soul.

Maybe you can teach me to wait,
To breathe through the moments.
And maybe I'll teach you to dance
In the flames of my passion.

Maybe we'll find a way to burn and flow.

Loving a Dream

Can you love a person without meeting them?
Maybe it's not the person we love,
But the possibility they represent,
The hope that somewhere, somehow,
There's a soul that fits with ours,
Even if we've never met.

Is it possible to love a dream?
To hold onto the idea of someone
As if they were already here,
Close enough to touch,
Yet forever out of reach.

I miss something I never had—
Staying up at night, lingering in the places
Between sleep and dream.

I miss the sound of laughter that never echoed,
And the touch of a hand that never held mine.

I wonder if it's possible to miss something
That doesn't exist

Almost

25

Almost… what a terrifying word.

I almost called.
You almost stayed.
Our love was almost enough….

I'm a Crier

I'm a crier. I've always been.

I cry for the sad things,
just as I do for the happy ones.
I cry over movies, music, art, ideas.

I cry because we never met,
and because sometimes I don't believe we will.

I also cry because maybe—just maybe—we might.
And I know life won't magically become perfect with you in it,
but I cry thinking how good it could be.

I'm a crier. I've always been.

I'm a Crier

Is Love Real?

Some days, I am afraid love might be just a
fragment of my imagination—
a lucid dream that feels so real, yet can never
be reached.

Is love simply a distant song
I heard once in another lifetime?

Some days, it feels like I'm trying to catch
sunlight with my palms.

Some days, I wonder if I made it all up.
I believed in promises of connection
that never found their way home.

Some nights,
I lie awake
searching for proof
that love is more than a beautiful lie
my heart keeps telling itself—

a dream I keep chasing,
believing that one day
it will finally be real.

Confession

I hate to admit it, but I, too, feel lonely some days.
I preach about independence, yet I cry alone,
hoping there was someone to wipe away those tears.

I hate to admit it, but I feel lonely some nights,
reaching out for the hand that isn't there.

I hate to admit it, but sometimes I just want to be held,
to be seen in my rawest form—unguarded and vulnerable,
to be loved not for my strength, but for my fragility, too.

The Fear

The scariest thing
is the possibility

that the person I so desperately need
exists only
in my head.

Fate

I believe in fate, in soulmates, and love.
So what if I haven't met mine?
So what if love has only burned me?
So what if I've only danced
with the ghosts of what could have been?

I've only known love that taught me sorrows,
but so what?
What if my heart has been
a battlefield of scars and ashes?

I still believe in warmth and soft embrace.
I believe in a love that won't set me aflame
but light my way home.

I believe in a love that will arrive
like the dawn after a long night.
Gentle but certain, unyielding and true—
a love that feels like finding home
in the eyes of another who sees me
and stays.
Unafraid of my fire and ashes.

*****

32

I miss you too much for us to never meet

I miss you too much for us to never meet

Home

"Lights will guide you home."

They tried,
but how do you find your way
back to something that doesn't exist?

They say home is where your heart is.

And my heart belongs to someone
I don't even know exists.

But if you are real,
maybe you can ask the lights
to guide me
to you…

September 23rd

I didn't have a good day, and I wish I could have told you all
about it. You'd give me a hug, and I'd feel better.

I wish you were here. I know we haven't met, but I wish you
were here.

If only I could tell you everything—
the weight of today, the ache of tomorrow—
and how I know, deep down,
you would understand it all without a single word.

I wish you were here.
And maybe, in some way, you already are.

Sometimes I look on Google maps,
searching for something that doesn't exist.

I walk the streets I once knew,
but the only ones walking them with me
are the ghosts of what never was.

My home was taken and
I never found a new one...

Matches in the Dark

Perhaps not all loves are meant to live.
Some are matches struck in the dark —
they flare,
they blind,
they warm your hands for a moment,
and then they are gone

Body

I gave my body to strangers,
not asking for anything in return.

I gave it easily, without question.

I gave them my body,
but never my heart—

not realizing
it was suffering all along,

breaking under the weight
of what I refused to feel,

aching for the love
I thought I didn't need

Exhausted

I'm exhausted.

Exhausted from waiting,
from getting my hopes up
only to watch them fall again.

Exhausted from crying into my pillow at night
and washing the stains away in the morning.

Exhausted from watching everyone succeed
and pretending I'm not jealous.
Exhausted from feeling guilty
for that jealousy too.

Exhausted from carrying dreams
too heavy for one heart to hold.

Exhausted from wanting so much
and ending up with so little.

Exhausted from hoping tomorrow will be better
and waking up to the same weight on my chest.

Exhausted from giving so much of myself
to a world that never seems to give back.

5 a.m.

Awake at 5 a.m., I stare at my phone.
Mourning the life I had.
Crying over it—
over places, people, feelings.
Referring to you as home,
while not knowing where home really is now—
or if it ever existed

Almost Right

Are you making promises to another,
wondering why it doesn't quite fit?

Are you holding onto a hand that feels foreign—
not because you don't want love,
but because you're not ready
for the one that fits just right?

Is it easier to stay in what feels safe
than to risk everything
for the one you're not yet ready to meet?

It's not that you don't feel.

It's that the right one demands a part of you
that's still healing—
a love you can't give
until you've learned to give it to yourself first.

And so, you wait
with someone who isn't quite wrong,

but isn't quite right either

Choose Me Wild

Maybe love is not about being tamed.

Maybe it's about being understood.
About being fought for.

And if you ever choose me,
I hope you choose me wild.

Choose Me Wild

Christmas

I don't miss a lot of things. I try not to think too much about the past. The past is the past, and it's the present we live in.

But I would be lying if I said I never think about those moments of innocence — my childhood, the simpler times when my family wasn't divided by death and by life.

Most of all, I miss Christmas.

I don't know if it's the chill in the air that affects me, or the longing for the kind of childish joy I no longer feel. I miss the arguing in my grandma's kitchen when all of us were cooking dinner. I miss the shows I used to put on for my family, where everyone clapped no matter how bad or good they were.

I miss my grandma's Christmas duck — and how much she hated cooking it. I miss the smell of the pine tree in the house and the cherry juice from the box. I used to love that juice. I miss watching TV around Christmas time. I even miss the holiday commercials.

I miss my grandparents. I miss my dad. I miss my dog.

I know it might sound silly, but I do. She was part of that innocence I'm never getting back.

And if I could relive a single moment, I would choose Christmas.

Any Christmas of my childhood. With all the arguing, the shows, the singing, the Christmas duck, the pine tree in the house. With my dog, my grandparents, and my dad.

Yes — if I could relive a moment, I would choose Christmas.

Where Does Love Go?

I asked myself, when we leave people, where does the love go?
When things end, feelings don't automatically disappear.
But love was always living inside of you.
And it never depended on the relationship lasting.
When the connection ends, love doesn't need the object anymore.
So as time passes, it loses its grip.
And slowly, before you even realize, it returns to you…

Strangers Again

There's nothing worse
than being strangers again—

yet knowing
every inch
of each other's soul.

I was a shot of espresso
but you were allergic to
caffeine

Maybe

Maybe I'm just insane.
It's quite possible, you know.
They say all the best ones are,
So I guess you are in luck.

Maybe I'm just insane,
But in my madness, I create—
Worlds, words, and wonders
That only the broken understand.

So if I'm crazy, let me be,
For in the wreckage of my mind
There's poetry, there's fire,
And maybe, just maybe,
There's a little piece of me
You'll come to love.

Imperfect Mess

There are times when I doubt I was made for love.

I'm impatient. I'm loud. I always have to have the last word.
I am far from perfect—if anything, "imperfect mess" would
suit me better than any other label.

And I wonder if that scares you.

But isn't love about finding someone who meets you there—
in that mess?
Someone who sees the impatience, the need to be right, the
flaws stitched with contradictions,
and still says, "I choose you"?

Some days,
I worry love is meant for those who fit neatly into boxes—
who speak softly,
who let go of arguments like they were made of smoke.

I am not that person.

But maybe love isn't about being easy.
Maybe it's a battlefield for the stubborn,
a playground for restless souls
who wear their scars like badges
and whose voices carry the weight of truth,
even when it's ugly.

Still a Believer

There, in the midst of chaos and silence,
I am.

Forever bound to question everything.

My trust was broken so many times
I've lost count—

yet I'm still a believer.

And I stood there,
wondering, how did I get so lucky?

How did I manage to find all
these beautiful people and share this journey
with them? What did I do to deserve
so much love, support and happiness?
And why do other people go a lifetime
without having it?

I stood there with tears in my eyes
as I read messages from people
I never met

The One Who Stays

We meet people every day, and yet most won't touch our lives. They won't leave their mark. We will probably forget their faces, and their names will escape our lips.

But then, one will come who'll change everything. Someone who will learn every inch of your body and love every piece of your soul.

Who will read your favorite books simply because you love them. Who will know your favorite song and play it for you. Who will bring you flowers on a random Tuesday, just to see you smile.

Someone who will remember how you take your coffee, the stories that make you laugh, and the dreams that make your eyes sparkle.

They will make you believe in magic again—the magic of finding someone who understands you without words. Someone who knows when to keep you close and when to let you fly.

Yes, we meet people every day. Most of them come into our lives and leave quietly.
But then, one will come who will stay…

Light in the Dark

53

The world can turn dark
from time to time.

Find someone
who will light your heart
and help it find its way
in the darkness.

Light in the Dark

Seen in Full

To be loved
is to be seen in full.

To be understood —
not in spite of what broke us,
but because of it

I Don't Need You to Survive

I would be lying if I said I need you to survive.

You aren't my other half, for I have always been whole.

I would be lying if I said I can't breathe when you are not near,
and that the world turns black and white.

I won't crumble without you.
I won't be incomplete, because I'm not made of missing parts.

I can walk this world alone;
I've done it before, and I'll do it again.
But knowing you're out there,
knowing I could reach for you
and find your hand waiting for mine—
that makes the journey sweeter,
makes the nights less lonely
and the mornings worth waking up for.

I would be lying if I said I need you to survive,
but I wouldn't be lying if I said I need you to truly live.

A Little Softness

And if someone asks about me,
long after my name has stopped living on your lips,

I hope saying it again
brings you
a little softness.

October

57

And then October came,
carrying the scent of change.
The leaves began to let go,
and so did I

In the Next Life

And if we aren't meant
to be together in this life,

I promise
I'll find you
in the next

In the Next Life

Keeper of Your Dreams

I will be the keeper of your dreams.
I will guard your heart, and I will love your soul.
I will be there when the world feels too heavy,
and I will stand with you in the storm.
In the noise, I will be your quiet, and in the silence,
I will be the calm that soothes your fears.
I will be your strength when you're tired and your shelter
when the skies turn gray.

Your dreams, your heart, your soul—
they are safe with me,
for I will love them as my own,
and I will be here, always,
in every breath, in every moment,
forever yours.

Getting Lost to Find You

I will find my way to you, just as I've found my way back to myself. You have to get lost in life to find your way.

And maybe it's through all those wrong turns and dead ends that we finally learn the right path. It's in those moments of confusion and doubt that we discover what we truly want, who we really are, and what we're willing to fight for.

Sometimes we have to wander through the darkness to appreciate the light. We have to get lost in order to understand what it means to be found, to know the difference between simply existing and truly living. And when I do find you, it won't be by chance but by choice, knowing that every step, every misstep, has led me here—to you.

November

November has always held a special hold over my heart, and not just because it's my birthday month, though I can't deny it has its perks. There's something magical about the air turning colder, the way your breath becomes visible, carrying warmth into the chill. And as the world cools down, a quiet kind of beauty emerges...

You Don't Have to Be Perfect

You don't have to be perfect to be loved.

Not for me.

I will love your broken heart
and your wounded soul.

You don't have to pretend to be better with me.

I will accept all the darkness inside you
and cherish it as much as your light.

You don't have to wear a mask,
hide parts of yourself,
or feel ashamed.

I will love you—
your imperfections,
your faults,
your mistakes.

You don't have to be perfect to be loved.

Not for me.

Travelers

We're all just travelers here,
making our way through the waves of life.
Sometimes, we get lucky enough
to share that journey with someone special—
and with the ordinary ones
who aren't so ordinary after all.

Sometimes, we have to go alone
to learn that we are strong enough
to stand firmly in the darkest of storms.
So when that special soul comes along,
we'll know—
not by how much we need them,
but by how free we feel walking beside them

Dancing in the Chaos

65

Maybe that's what it is all about—
Finding another imperfect person
Who will dance in the chaos of life with you.

Dancing in the Chaos

In Another Timeline

Today was a good day, and once again, I find myself wishing
you were here to hear all about it. I should probably warn you—
I'm a talker. But in my mind, so are you.
I imagine us talking late into the night, never tiring of
interrupting each other mid-conversation, yet always
remembering the smallest details about one another.
In my head, we've already met. Maybe we did. If not in this
timeline, then in another. Perhaps over there, we live in the
countryside, growing tomatoes and drinking wine for lunch.
I like to picture it. Some days, though, I'm unsure—unsure if all
the signs I see are real, or just my imagination.
But even if it's just a dream, it's a comforting one.
And for now, that's enough.

"I Love You" is in Many Things

"I love you" is in the morning kisses,
In the way hands find each other under the table.

It exists in the patience of waiting,
In the shared silence when words are not needed.

"I love you" is in the gentle way someone tucks a stray hair
behind your ear,
And in the laughter that fills the room.

It's in the sacrifice made without hesitation,
And in the hug that shields you from the world.

"I love you" lives in the smallest gestures
 and in the grandest commitments.
"I love you" is in the everyday and in the extraordinary.

This Chapter

Maybe this chapter of my life
is the one where I find myself.

Or maybe it's the one
where I stop looking
and just live

Silly Girl

Silly girl, you almost forgot:
You are the ray of sunshine on a rainy day.
You are the breath of fresh air,
The symphony, the bloom in a garden of gray.
Silly girl, don't you see?
You are the masterpiece in plain sight

Proof That Love Exists

I know love exists.

I know it because I have my friends.

The ones who say,
"Text me when you get home,"
and then call
when the message doesn't come.

The ones who bring flowers
on ordinary Tuesdays
because I said I was having a hard day.

The ones who take me out for matcha,
even though they hate it,
just to sit across from me
while I unravel.

The ones who let me talk for hours
about the same ache,
never rushing me,
never shrinking me,
never making me feel like I am too much.

I know love exists
because I have felt it
in voice notes sent at midnight,
in hands reaching across tables,
in silence that doesn't need to be filled.

Romantic love may arrive and leave.
But this,
this kind of love —
stays.

And if that is not proof
that love is real,
I don't know what is.

June, 2025

I think, more than anything, I just want to be *known*. Truly, deeply known. I want someone to see the parts of me I try to hide, the quiet sadness, the chaos, the flaws, and not look away. I want them to step into the darkest corners of my heart and still find light there. Still find me.

I want someone who wants to hear it all. The things I write, the ideas I obsess over, the thoughts that come at 2 a.m. Someone who doesn't flinch, doesn't judge, doesn't get tired of me being too much.

I want to write them letters, long and messy and honest. I want to cook their favorite meal just to see the way their eyes light up. And I want to lie there, quietly, while they read to me from their favorite book, not because it's mine, but because it's theirs, and that makes it matter to me.

How do you explain that you just want to be known?

Special to Me

You aren't special.
And neither am I.

The world is full of people like us —
those who wake up every day
promising to change their lives tomorrow,
and those for whom
"tomorrow" never comes.

We aren't special
to the world.

But maybe that was never the point.

Because you are special
to me.

And I am special
to you.

And sometimes,
that is enough.

Found Me in Your Eyes

Love searched for me
time and time again,
and I hid from it.

I fear it may have finally found me
in your eyes.

And then I realized,
It was always me.
I was the one changing,
Not the world around...
The world has stayed
the same...

Temple

My love is a temple
And my heart is a heaven.
My soul is a sanctuary,
Where the light of truth burns eternal.

Temple

I Wish I Could Hate You

I wish I could hate you.

How much easier that would be.

I wish I could make you the villain
and file our story into the darkest corner of my mind,
never to revisit again.

But that wouldn't be fair.

I wish I could feel resentment
every time your name crosses my thoughts.

But I don't...

I Am Not Broken

I am not broken.
I am not a fragile object that easily cracks at the first blow.
I've known pain, and I've known sadness.
Grief hasn't escaped me either.
I've been lied to and used; I've been played but not shattered.
I am not a fragile object to be cast aside, only to be looked at.

I am not broken.
I'm not someone who needs to be saved, nor am I someone who
has to be fixed.

I do not need to be mended or made whole,
For I am already enough—
As I am, as I've been, as I will be.

I am not broken;
I am simply becoming.

When I Arrive

Someone out there is waiting—
waiting for me to arrive.

Perhaps in Berlin,
Tokyo,
or Amsterdam.
Maybe even in Quebec.

As I pack my bags,
I think of them.

As I close this chapter and leave,
I look forward
to meeting them
when I arrive.

You Will Be Loved

I wish you knew how loved you'd be—by people who haven't yet entered your life.
I wish I could tell you. I know you think you will never belong.
You are scared people will forever look at you and see an odd little creature.
And I wish you could hear me when I say it's not true.

I wish I could show you the future, the one where you are surrounded by misunderstood souls who love you for your oddness.
The ones who bring out the quirks you tried so hard to hide away.

I wish you knew there is a whole world waiting for you out there, ready to accept, cherish, and love your uniqueness.

You feel small now, like you're fading into the background of everyone's life, but there's a day coming when you'll shine so brightly that you'll be impossible to ignore.
It's not because you'll change into something new, but because you'll finally see yourself the way I do.

I wish I could tell you how loved you'd be. But you'll learn it yourself soon.

I Know What I Want

I know what I want. Is that so bad?
I'm looking for love. Boring, steady,
the "I choose you in every universe" kinda love.
I want someone who wants me in every waking moment,
even at my lowest, even when I don't want myself.
I know what I want.
I want to be seen, to be cared for,
to hand over my whole heart
without fear it will be dropped.
I know what I want… is that so bad?

I Know What I Want

I Was Never A Summer Girl

I was never a summer girl—
With shiny hair that always looked flawless,
Or a smile that brightened someone's day.
I was never the ray of sunshine,
And no one called me "the life of the party" either.
I was never a summer girl.

I am messy.
I am someone who will always spill a drink on a white shirt,
Someone who laughs too loud and forgets the punchline of her own joke,
Someone who wears mismatched socks and always talks a lot.

I am a rainy day with a cozy sweater,
A hot cup of tea, and a book that smells like it's been loved a little too much.

No, I am not a summer girl—
I am the calm after a storm,
The quiet that comes when the world has stopped spinning.
I am the gray skies and the steady rhythm of raindrops,
The comfort of knowing that not every day
 has to be bright to be beautiful

I Was Never A Summer Girl

Maybe That's the Point

Maybe we will never know
what life was all about.

And maybe that's the whole point.

Maybe our only purpose
is to simply live—

make mistakes,
learn from them,
go to new places,
evolve,
create,
love.

Maybe life is a journey,
not the destination
after all….

My Final Act of Love

And when this story becomes something we used to be,
my final act of love
will be wishing you the courage
to see yourself
the way I always did —
worthy, whole, enough.

Spring

It's almost spring.

The birds are singing outside my bedroom window,
and my soul is singing in unison with them.

Life is suddenly
worth living again.

The Beauty of Being Human

Oh, the beauty of being human.

The warmth of a hug.
A good cry over a song that hits a little too close.

The first kiss…
and all the ones that follow.

A shared laugh.
A dance in the middle of the street.

The food that tastes like home.

The sunrises you meet alone,
wrapped in a blanket.

The sunsets you meet
with the ache of missing someone —
and loving them anyway.

Oh, the chaos
and the wonder
of being human.

May Love Find You Gently

I hope the next time love finds you,
it will be in the form of someone
who chooses you,
over and over and over again.

I hope it finds you in a gentle heart,
one that's afraid of losing you.

And I hope the next time love finds you,
it arrives not as chaos,
but as peace.

May Love Find You Gently

And in the end,
I found that home
was never something
I was missing

Home

And in the end, I have finally learned
that home is not a place.
Not a city.
Not a house with warm lights in the windows.

It is not even a person,
no matter how much I once wished it were.

Home is not something we chase across countries,
or search for in someone else's arms.

Home is ourselves.

Wherever you are,
I hope you feel at home...

www.ingramcontent.com/pod-product-compliance
Lightning Source LLC
Chambersburg PA
CBHW021339060726
47591CB00006B/2094